Wheels around Kirkcaldy and

Alan Brotchie

Always a delight to look out for any rail journey through Burntisland were the diminutive 'pug' engines which shunted the sidings of the British Aluminium Company. The first, seen here, was purchased when the facility was under construction in 1915, supplied (unusually for Scotland) by Peckett & Sons of Bristol. In their later years, all three were painted bright green and kept in immaculate condition. Fortunately, after they became redundant in the 1970s, all were taken into preservation. Now the aluminium works has gone, the large site has become a colony of bijou dwellings which could look just as comfortable in St. Albans or Milton Keynes as on the shores of Fife.

Text © Alan Brotchie, 2010.
First published in the United Kingdom, 2010,
by Stenlake Publishing Ltd.
Telephone: 01290 551122
www.stenlake.co.uk

ISBN 9781840334982

Acknowledgements

The provision of photographs in this selection was assisted by Eric Eunson, Bill Fiet, the late Robert Grieves, Allan Rodgers, Martin Rodgers, Bill Todd and Pete Westwater, to all of whom I must record my sincere gratitude.

A North British Railway Edinburgh express of the Edwardian era exits Kinghorn tunnel and passes a group of linesmen standing back from the track. The tunnel is still a delaying factor on the East Coast Main Line, with a speed restriction of 30 mph for trains passing through. It was constructed from both ends simultaneously, but did not meet exactly as planned. The consequent 'kink' still exists, hence the speed restriction. In the foreground is the steep branch down to Pettycur Harbour which served coke ovens, and later a bottle works which initially used sand from the beach in the manufacturing process.

Introduction

East Fife may be defined as that geographic part of Fife which historically looked to Kirkcaldy as its trade centre. Fife perhaps suffered from having too many such 'centres' with not only Kirkcaldy, but Dunfermline and the county town of Cupar. In recent years this confusion has been overcome by the New Town of Glenrothes being the locus chosen for location of new centralised council departments. To some 'East Fife' conjures up the eponymous football team – the pride of Methil – but for many years, 1885 to 1983, it was a Parliamentary Constituency famous as the seat of the Liberal Prime Minister, H H Asquith.

This eastern area of Fife was, until the commencement of coal exploitation on an industrial scale in the nineteenth century, something of a physical, cultural and transportation backwater. Communication was hardly necessary, or even encouraged, and the area assumed a distant air of 'remoteness' which was enhanced by its relative physical isolation from most of the remaining part of the country of Scotland. Kings, their retinues and courts came and went to a smattering of royal palaces and hunting lodges, the roads of the middle ages being fit for this irregular use, and for the occasional packman and horse with basic necessities for the rural population. Any bulk commodities were transported around the long coastline by small sailing ships, their tonnages limited by the restrictive size of the harbours. Early plans of Fife (the first of which dates back to circa 1679), show few roads and those which are indicated almost invariably lie in a north – south direction across Fife's isthmus between the Firths of Forth and Tay. These basic lines of communication served the agricultural and ecclesiastical needs of the area until the dawn of the Industrial Revolution, when both imports and exports demanded improved distribution. The first designated turnpike roads in Fife were defined by Act of Parliament in 1753, including the Great North Road between North Queensferry and Perth. However, it was not until an Act of 1790 that the turnpike system was extended throughout the eastern parts of the county. Already by this date the first wooden-railed waggonways had been constructed in the Kingdom to carry coal from mines located inland to the shipping ports on the coast. Early examples in this area were to be found at Kirkcaldy, Wemyss, Leven and Pittenweem. There was also a proposal in 1835, related to planned improvements for Pettycur Harbour, to construct a horse drawn passenger tramway thence, by Kinghorn, along the coast to Kirkcaldy. This would have been the first passenger tramway in Scotland, but this advanced idea never progressed beyond the planning stage.

Further improvements came with the construction of main line railways through the area. The earliest of these, the Edinburgh and Northern Railway, opened from Burntisland (where it connected to the world's first train carrying ferry boats) through Kirkcaldy to Cupar in September 1847 and on to Ferryport on Tay (the later Tayport) the following May. Soon north and east Fife were well covered by branch and main lines offering links to all major destinations. Mineral traffic was served by a network of private lines, the best remembered of these being the Wemyss Private Railway which carried the coal mined at the Wemyss collieries to Methil Docks or the central washing plant. This eventually amounted to several miles in length, and gave sterling service until June 1970.

Road transport development followed a fairly predictable pattern; sparse operation of horse buses gave way in the conurbations to electric tramways, with the Wemyss area having its 'mustard boxes', as their trams were nick-named, operating from Kirkcaldy to Leven until 1932. By this time most stage carriage operation was in the hands of a multitude of bus operators who were rapidly absorbed into the railway-funded Alexander's bus monopoly. Only in recent years, with the preponderance of journeys being made by private car, has the roads network of the area changed radically. While the region has no motorways, completion of the dual carriageway East Fife regional road in the late 1980s transformed journey time in the east to west direction, fulfilling plans aired fifty years previously.

Pettycur beach in June 1933 was witness to a remarkable sight, when an aircraft took off for the Isle of Man. The air taxi facility had just been started by a division of the Scottish Motor Transport Company, and this flight was booked by bus pioneer Bill Milne, co-founder, with Bill McLean of the Kelty Motor Transport Co. Milne had great belief in the future of air travel, at one time considering the purchase of a Tiger Moth. This aircraft, new to the SMT Co (note the company diamond logo on the tail fin) a De Havilland Rapide Dragon 1, had seats for six passengers. On this occasion Milne hired the plane to take himself and his wife and four guests to attend the Isle of Man TT races. Remarkably this seventy five year old flying machine still exists, and is currently being restored – hopefully to airworthy condition – in the south of England.

One of Bill McLean's first motor buses was this Maudslay, SP5183, purchased in 1920. The right hand side of the small garage behind his home in Oakfield Street was occupied by his Hallford charabanc. With these two vehicles a service was operated from Dunfermline to Kelty via Kingseat and Lassodie. The business prospered, and with no fewer than seventeen vehicles, was taken over by W Alexander & Sons in September 1931. Kelty was a hot spot for early bus operations, with no fewer than five distinct operators working from what was at that time a large mining village.

Kinghorn's High Street in the pre Second World War era was almost devoid of traffic – just one car on the left, and a horse lorry making a delivery to the grocers on the right. The architecture of the main street of the ancient Royal Burgh (given its Charter by King Alexander III in the thirteenth century) was spoiled by the council's attempt at improving the housing stock with an intrusive and unsympathetic 'block-house' of flats at the far north end of the street. Despite this, there remain some attractive old buildings in the town, although an unfortunate number, like Cuinzie Nook on the left, are falling into disrepair. ['Cuinzie' is said to refer to coins or coinage – but I prefer to think of it as 'Cosy Nook'!]

The Burgh of Kirkcaldy built an electric tramway running the length of what had been given the nickname of the 'Lang Toun', basically the original built-up area following the main road through the town from one end to the other from Linktown to Gallatown, a distance of just over 3 miles. The tramway opened on 28th February 1902, and was followed by extensions, which ultimately brought the total length to slightly over six miles. The western terminus was here in Links Street, where car 17 is seen in the 1920s, the spectators probably finding the photographer a more unusual spectacle than the tramcar. None of these old houses with typical crow-stepped gables remain today. The tramway lasted only until 15th May 1931, the council having decided to replace their trams by buses operated by Messrs Alexander.

The Kirkcaldy Links Market, a venerable institution and still the longest street fair in the world, was ousted from its original venue, Links Street, by the arrival of the trams. It moved a few yards south, to the parallel Sands Road which ran along and just above the high water line. The showmen who frequented the market with their stalls and rides used, until recently, a variety of fascinating vehicles to transport their equipment from one venue to the next. Highly prized were old Tilling-Stevens petrol-electric buses which used a petrol engine to drive an electric motor which powered the assemblage. Here, at the Links Market of the 1920s is a fascinating old steam lorry (registration U 1387), manufactured by 'Mann's Patent Steam Cart & Wagon Co Ld' of Leeds, and owned at that time by J Graham of Tollcross, Edinburgh. It may be the man himself at the steering wheel, with his family on the roof of the vehicle. Note also the 'decorative' grenade on the smoke box door!

A Kirkcaldy railway often overlooked was this temporary line, built by the contractor reconstructing Sands Road into the sea wall and esplanade. Sir Robert McAlpine & Son (Concrete Bob) was the main contractor for the scheme, which was undertaken as an unemployment alleviation project. Started in March 1922 it was completed the following year. The line was connected to sidings at Kirkcaldy Harbour, and was used for the transport of most of the necessary materials. The small locomotive can be identified as McAlpine's number 11 – a four wheeled saddle tank, built by Hudswell Clarke of Leeds in 1899, and previously used on McAlpine's other major contract in Fife, construction of Methil No. 3 Dock.

At Kirkcaldy Harbour the Corporation provided cranes to unload and load shipping and after 1912, this dimunitive, even for that era, saddle tank pug locomotive. It was purchased for £372 from Andrew Barclay, Sons & Co Ltd in March of that year, but had been built much earlier – probably in 1874 by Fletcher, Jennings & Co of Whitehaven in Cumbria. It seems to have been little used after the early 1920s and was completely out of use by the end of the Second World War. It lay rusting away on one of the harbour sidings at the East Pier for a few years longer, until cut up there for scrap in 1948.

Kirkcaldy, as one of the main population centres of Fife, played an early part in the development of motor bus services. Several nearby towns, not on the main rail network, found the advantages of bus links considerable. One of the very earliest companies established was the General Motor Carrying Company, founded by brothers-in-law Alex Sturrock and John McGregor in 1913. Their first regular service was to Kinghorn and Burntisland (a route which was actualy served by the railway). Many of their earliest vehicles were named after local castles. This scene, posed in front of a GMC charabanc (probably either of Caledon or Commer make) is about to set off with the annual choir outing from Sinclairtown Parish Church (now Viewforth Church) identifiable by its narrow diamond paned and pointed windows.

After a period of little progress during the First World War, the GMC expanded rapidly. Needless to say it suffered competition on many routes, and to counter this purchased small 'chaser' buses, Fords and, as seen here, Chevrolets. These were more expensive than the model 'T' Ford, but the extra cost was considered worth it in terms of reliability. SP8883 was bought new in May 1924, and is seen in Thistle Street, where the original garage and workshop were situated. Note the bulb horn which passes through the windscreen. The board indicates that the bus is operating on the Dunfermline route.

Many individuals bought small buses and charabancs, either to try to cream some of the trade from busy routes or to offer tours. This was at a time when it was said that there were people living in Gallatown who had never visited Kirkcaldy High Street. The availability of inexpensive transport was to change that for ever. This Reo SP9968 was the property of Johnny Westwater of Dysart, a taxi proprietor, whose sole bus this was, seen here about to depart with a touring party.

Two remarkable Sentinel steam lorries being delivered to Modern Roadways Ltd, established in 1932 with a head office in Market Street, Kirkcaldy. The company was founded by a mining engineer, James Mason. It had but a brief existence, being put into voluntary liquidation in September 1936, and was wound up three months later. The massive pneumatic tyred Sentinel vehicles (built in Shrewsbury, although the company was established in Glasgow) probably represented the highest development of steam road traction. The Road Traffic Act of 1930 deliberately penalised this form of traction, basing road tax upon axle loading, supposedly to ensure that road maintenance was equably apportioned. This was compounded the following year by an increase in road tax for road locomotives to £100 pa allied with a reduction in fuel oil tax. The outcome was to effectively drive steam haulage off the roads.

Wheeled transport making through the gates of the Beveridge Park in Kirkcaldy. The 104 acre park, gifted to the citizens of the town by former provost Michael Beveridge in 1892, also had a tram line built up to the gates. This proved to be a severe financial disappointment, and it saw little regular service. It came into its own however when Raith Rover's home matches were played at Stark's Park, when trams waited here to take supporters home. The park is a much-prized asset today, and is home to a miniature railway track, where members of the Kirkcaldy Model Railway Society can operate their model locomotives. This 200 yard long line has facility for 3½, 5, and 7¼ inch gauge operation. The park was also home for forty years from 1948 to Scotland's first motorcycle road races, which thereafter moved to the purpose-built circuit at Knockhill.

This steam thrashing mill at Templehall Farm, is at the top of Hendry Road, Kirkcaldy in the 1920s. The traction engine was to drive the thrasher, with women assisting, feeding the opened sheaves into the mill. Kirkcaldy expanded rapidly to the north west after 1930 and Templehall became a large council housing scheme in the 1950s. No trace whatsoever remains of the old farm steading. The name Templehall is considered by some to have a direct connection with the Knights Templar, but locally it has become associated with one of the several peripheral estates, constructed in the fifties, with little provision of amenities or necessary social requirements.

Looking east along Links Street, Kirkcaldy in the 1940s. The massive gas holder, retort house and chimney of the Municipal Gas Works are long gone, but at that time they cast a malevolent brooding presence over this part of the town. The double deck Alexander's Guy approaching is painted in the red livery which distinguished the buses used on the town services, a feature shared with Perth (in both cases replacing the former municipal tram service). The bus is passing the 1938 Raith Cinema, a distinctive building which still exists, now serving as the Rhema Church Centre. Virtually all of the buildings on the south side of the street have been replaced.

Traffic is building up in this late 1920s scene at the foot of Whytescauseway in Kirkcaldy at its junction with the High Street. Tram rails and overhead are still in place, but soon the tramway would be abandoned. The white-gloved policeman, perhaps supposedly on points duty, does not appear too involved, merely observing the motor cycle combination with sidecar and the preceding Morris to make their way towards the west (or south!) end of the town. McBean's shop on the corner was replaced by a striking three store storey Burton's gentleman's outfitters in 1935.

Kirkcaldy's quiet High Street in the 1940s with another of Alexander's angular red painted Guy double deckers on town service 6. The bus is passing one of the few (as there were then) branches of Marks and Spencer – its clock conveniently telling us that the time is 1.45 pm. This branch opened in 1937, the first in the east of Scotland, with people even travelling specially from as far afield as Edinburgh for the privilege of shopping here! The store was built on the site of the former Town House of the Burgh, which stood here from 1827 until 1935; the replacement Town House in Wemyssfield, although started in 1937, was not completed until 1956.

The esplanade and sea wall, completed in 1923, can be seen to good effect in this view some twelve years later. The area between the road and the sea wall has not yet been given over to car parking, and the utilitarian 'country' bus station at the foot of Charlotte Street is yet to make an appearance. All the buildings on the landward side have now gone. The bus prominent in the foreground is a brand new Alexander's Bluebird Leyland TS7, registered AFG in Fife, and showing 'Perth' as its destination. Many of these vehicles were converted to double deckers during the Second World War and ran until about 1960. The skyline in the distance of Pathhead is one of linoleum factories and chimneys, a scene transformed, following the construction in 1964-5 of the three blocks of fifteen storey flats.

Before its move to Invertiel, Alexander's bus workshop and paint shop was to be found in the Oswald Road, Gallatown former tram depot of Kirkcaldy Corporation. This (mostly) happy group of employees was photographed there in mid-1946. The double deck bus behind is RO482, one of the stalwarts of the fleet at that time. A Guy Arab, it was supplied in July 1944, registration number AMS154, and lasted in service until 1967. It, and many of its contemporaries, was then purchased for scrapping by T Muir and languished for some time in his yard on the Thornton Road. Muir also took over this building in Oswald Road, and after standing derelict for some years after he vacated it, the red sandstone faced structure was demolished.

A scene at Kirkcaldy Harbour with the two steam cranes unloading cork for the linoleum industry. One of these cranes was built by William Morgan & Coy of Kilwinning in Ayrshire and outlasted the Corporation's small pug engine by many years. Kirkcaldy Corporation had hopes of their harbour being used for coal export, but this never materialised to any extent, the facilities at Burntisland (downstream) and Methil (upstream) being, in normal circumstances, more than adequate. The harbour remained busy, however, dealing mostly with imports and exports relating to the floor cloth industry. It was closed to shipping in 1992, the last use being during the previous year.

The rail approach to Kirkcaldy Harbour was one of the steepest in Great Britain (to be worked by adhesion only) at 1:21, and was originally operated by a stationary engine hauling wagons up attached to a cable. Eventually in the mid-19th century this was abandoned, and locomotive use took over. However, on at least two occasions the whole train ran away out of control, ending in the cold waters of the harbour. Here, in November 1954, the services of the breakdown crane are called for to extricate the harbour pug, class J88 number 68341 from the depths, after it had attempted, but failed, to bring down the line a train with seven wagons more than was (for good reason) stipulated. Considering the difficulties of normal operation of the steep branch, the manoeuvring of the breakdown equipment down the line must have presented considerable difficulty.

Perhaps surprisingly, there appear to be no happy faces when the latest in transport technology reaches the separate Burgh of Dysart for the first time in January 1911. The mile-long branch from the main line at Pathhead was the final addition to the Kirkcaldy Corporation's tramway system. The Dysart terminus was outside the Parish Church, where the track was built hard against the footpath, rather than the conventional position in the middle of the street, so as to create minimum obstruction. At one time it had been hoped that the line would extend up Normand Road as far as the 'White Gates' level crossing, and that a line from there would connect to the Wemyss tramway, but this never came to pass. On the day that the Dysart line opened (26th January) takings amounted to £4.10. 0d; with the fare set at 1d, this represented just over one thousand tickets sold.

Below: This fine Daimler car was owned by the proprietors of Dysart's Royal Hotel, brother and sister, Alex and Maggie Shand, presumably the proud occupants of the vehicle. The nineteenth century building in the Townhead, opposite the Parish Church, is still a popular privately owned hotel serving the twenty first century.

Right: The fiercely independent burgh of Dysart retained its independence until 1930, and the "Saut Burgh" still has a distinct air of separation from its larger neighbour to the west. This 1930s scene of the High Street is from the Cross, looking towards the trees surrounding Dysart House, once the seat of General James St. Clair and much later purchased by linoleum magnate Sir Michael Nairn. He gave much of the estate (Ravenscraig Park) to the citizens of Kirkcaldy in 1896. The house has been a Carmelite nunnery since 1931. These charming old houses were swept away in the 1960s; the only building in the scene which still exists is the single storey one behind the milk cart. Farms delivered milk in churns, customers taking their own jugs to be filled.

June 1920 at Thornton Junction and the North British Railway locomotive 'Glen Gloy', number 35, is probably newly delivered from the NB's Cowlairs Works. From the right, fireman J Stobie at the cab door, Shedmaster J Ellis, Running Foreman W Simpson, Inspector John Allan, driver Thomson and in his Sunday best, Inspector Allan's son. Thornton was an important railway junction, a central amalgamation point for much of the county's coal production transport. It had a station, about a mile from the village centre, a locomotive shed and wagon repair shops; very much a railway community. The connection continues, as Thornton is now home to John Cameron's main line steam locomotives, including the A4 pacific 'Union of South Africa'. 'Glen Gloy' served for forty years, being scrapped in June 1960; another of the same class, 'Glen Douglas' has been preserved.

Below: Just three miles to the north-east of Thornton is the small town, or large village, of Markinch, which has now become almost a suburb of Glenrothes. For many years the main employer was the Haig's whisky distillery, but this has now closed. If it were not for the thoughtfulness of the sender of this card on 12th November 1903, we would be in total ignorance of the nature of the event taking place. However, we are advised by J Calley that "This is the procession of the store when it was opened on the 4th October. Hope you got home all right ..." So this is a view of the opening of the Markinch Co-operative Department Store in the High Street. All of these buildings have since been replaced by modern housing.

Left: At Thornton Junction locomotive shed in the wartime years many tasks were undertaken by women, replacing men on active service. The locomotive is a 'Great Central' type 2-8-0 of which several were based in Fife for use on heavy coal trains, prior to the arrival later during the war of the 'Austerity' type. Note the white painted borders to aid visibility during the hours of black-out.

Still in Markinch High Street, this scene is photographed immediately across the street from the previous view; in this case the pend and building still remain, although no longer a shop. This fine study of the butcher's cart belonging to John Miller is by William Aitken, outside whose place of business the conveniently posed view was recorded. Other examples of his work are on display in the window. Markinch was also home to another pioneer photographer, John Terras, a prolific and gifted recorder of the local scene who founded a business in 1880. He recorded many local events, possibly including the one on the previous page. The Terras photography business still exists, still under family ownership in the twenty first century.

John Patrick of Leven was another of the pioneer Fife photographers. Although he advertised in his promotional literature that the business was founded in 1853, the photographic side probably dated from circa 1866. It was probably his son, James, who continued the business, that recorded a series of views along the new Wemyss tramways at the end of September 1906. As the Wemyss line was initially short of cars they hired three cars from the Kirkcaldy tramways to augment their stock. This is one of these Kirkcaldy trams seen at North Lodge, where the line left the highway to go cross country to Coaltown of Wemyss. After cessation of tram operation, this was a favourite venue for (illegal) 'pitch and toss' gambling schools.

This fine composition by John Terras of Markinch was made very early in the life of the Wemyss tramways. The card was posted on 6th September 1906 – the tramway was only opened two weeks previously! The local children of Coaltown of Wemyss are still enthralled by the novelty, but this was soon to evaporate. After a serious accident the tramway running through Main Street was abandoned and a replacement was built behind the village.

This delivery van from the West Wemyss Co-operative Society doing its rounds is seen at the Lower Cottages of Lochhead Farm. Founded in 1852, at a time when many such societies were established, the West Wemyss Co-op retained its identity until 1922, when it merged with the nearby Dysart society. This in its turn became part of the Central and East Fife society in 1971, and is still a small part of the Co-operative Wholesale Society (CWS)

Gathering in the harvest and building it into stacks at Lochhead Farm in the 1920s, with carts bringing the crop to the stack yard. The triangular wooden fabrication lying on the ground is a centre former, which when erected, forms the centre around which the stack is built. These were usually lifted above ground level on stone staddles to keep the crop out of the reach of damp and vermin.

Merryweather & Sons of Greenwich, which was established as far back as 1692, manufactured this new fire engine purchased by Buckhaven and Methil, the *Fire King*, one of the very first self-propelled fire engine designs, seen here being tested in 1909 at the East Pier. It cost £1200, a very considerable sum, and was kept operational until 1931. To demonstrate its reliability, it was driven from Hawick to Buckhaven; one can only admire the fortitude of the driver who was assigned to this task! The engine carried a very odd registration number – A.1.KJ, with lettering on a white plate, rather than the conventional way. When numbers were introduced in 1903, several issuing authorities had strange quirky ideas of their own (for example Aberdeenshire – RS – had a series RS.X for some buses and other commercial vehicles). All these idiosyncrasies were eventually rationalised.

This occasion is an outing for the members of the choir of Buckhaven United Free Church. The building stood on the west side of Church Street and resembled the Parish Church architecturally, but has since been demolished and the site is now occupied by housing. After being deconsecrated, the building was used for a time by Remploy as a clothing factory, until this facility was removed to new premises in Leven.

The Wellesley Colliery Brass Band posing in Denbeath in one of the Tramway Company's Tilling-Stevens TS3A charabancs which had a 25 seat body built by Strachan & Brown of London. The band was formed in 1919, but the photo probably dates from just after June1924 when the charabanc (SP9168) was newly purchased (it was soon altered to pneumatic tyres to replace its original bone-shaking solid tyres). The band was successful in competitions, winning the Scottish Championships in 1944. In 1976 it amalgamated with the Buckhaven Town Band, and is still blowing strong.

Below: Methil Docks were where most of the output from the Wemyss Collieries was shipped for export, the estate having a large influence on the design and development of the facilities. While an early dock was constructed by the forward-looking estate management, development of the facility was later in the hands of the North British Railway Company and served the needs of other Fife collieries. On the left is a wagon from the Dundonald Coal Company, Cardenden, which was purchased in 1909 by the Lochgelly Iron & Coal Company. The locomotive in the centre belonged to the Wemyss Coal Company, one of two built in 1904 by the North British Locomotive Company of Glasgow.

Left: Before the establishment of the National Health Service on 5th July 1948 under the leadership of the Health Minister, Aneurin (Nye) Bevan, healthcare was frequently financed by local trusts and voluntary contributions. Fund-raising was an annual preoccupation, with flag days, fetes and other charitable events. This fine picture is of "Annie" from St. Agnes, Methil. As St. Agnes was the nurse's home serving the Randolph Wemyss Memorial Hospital in Wellesley Road, Buckhaven, it seems a not unreasonable conclusion that Annie was a nurse, and she and her bicycle were doing their bit for a fund-raising competition.

Construction of the third coal dock at Methil, the photo dating from 5th November 1908. The two earlier facilities were quickly found to be too small for the ever-increasing size of the coal handling vessels. Hence Methil No. 3 dock was planned and built, with a considerable degree of reticence by the North British Railway. These doubts proved to be accurate, and the extensive (and expensive) dock became a white elephant, never operating at full capacity. It was closed to shipping in 1977, and has since been partially filled.

The Wemyss Coal Company had a training school for lads at Muiredge Pit. However, in the 1930s there was no guarantee of a job when your time at the school was completed. Here a class is taught the 'safe' manner to couple two hutches together. The risk to life, and particularly to limb, is very apparent. These operations had perforce to take place in the dangerous working environment of the pit, with noisy and frequently dark conditions.

Below: This scene has been identified as being in the old part of Buckhaven, probably the old High Street. Before the arrival of coal mining in a major sense after the second half of the nineteenth century, the main industry of this small town was fishing, and there can be little doubt that the fish on sale from the cart would be fresh – probably caught the previous day in the Forth. Fishing at that time was inshore, unlike the situation now, when the few Scottish boats which still fish are often at sea for several days at a time. From a fleet of over ninety fishing smacks at the end of the 1870s, in the next forty years this reduced to five boats. The harbour soon became unusable, being filled with sea-washed 'redd' from nearby coal bings, where colliery waste was merely tipped into the sea.

Right: With the coming of the Nationalisation of the coal industry in 1947, the new NCB attempted to acquire the railway which linked the pits of the former Wemyss Coal Company to the docks and central coal washing plant. This move was, however, resisted by the Company, and eventually this line was deemed not to be part of the NCB, and was run by a committee including the estate. The Wemyss Private Railway, as it then became, earned a good return for the estate until, following the virtual eclipse of coal working in the area it was closed on 26th June 1970. Its locomotives, most painted a chocolate colour, were larger than the normally found colliery 'pug'. Several of them have been preserved.

Methil High Street had, unsurprisingly for a busy sea port, a large number of public houses. This is Campbell's Steamboat Tavern at the foot of Fisher Street, an unusual building for this part of Scotland, being constructed in brick. The proprietor has sent this postcard, saying, "What do you think of our Landau and pair?" He has enabled us to date the scene fairly precisely, as in the window of the Tavern is a poster advertising an event on Saturday 12th November 1904, and the postmark is dated 23rd November. The building no longer exists.

This Morris Commercial lorry belonging to Alex Anderson, contractor of Methilhill is being used as a float promoted by the local Boys' Brigade detachment, again possibly to raise hospital funds. The Boys' Brigade was founded in Glasgow by William Smith in 1883, and is the oldest such uniformed organisation. On the cab roof of the lorry is displayed the Brigade's anchor symbol, with the motto 'Sure & Stedfast'. Although this is the original and accepted spelling, some companies prefer to use the alternative spelling 'Steadfast'. The photo dates from after 1926, as the anchor emblem displayed has added the cross of the Boys' Life Brigade, the organisations having merged in that year.

A 1955 view looking west along Methil High Street, taken from the railway bridge which carried the lines down from the pits at Aberhill to the docks, a very steep and sharply curved line which always felt as if there was an accident waiting to happen. It is worthy of note that all the motor vehicles on the street were made in Britain, also that the photographer has been spotted by several of the shopkeepers and bystanders who are perhaps waiting to ensure that they are recorded for posterity. On the corner of the building on the right there is a traditional barber's pole, one of the very few trader's insignia which still remain to be seen today. Its red and white stripes are said to represent the blood spilt when shaving with an open razor was practised, and the white bandages used to stem the flow!

Leven attracted several industries, amongst them Henry Balfour's Durie Foundry which had a high reputation for large castings and plant for town gas works. This boiler, en route from Leven, was actually photographed near Tillicoultry as it made its slow and tortuous journey to Grangemouth. One has to wonder if it would not have been possible to ship the load, and take it a much more direct route by sea. Leven had a harbour, but by this date it had possibly silted up to such a degree as to prevent a suitably sized vessel from gaining access. The two traction engines were most likely owned by A & R Brown of Colinsburgh. It was not unknown for loads of this magnitude to destroy culverts under the roads.

Leven Station in 1912 with the Fife Coast Express. This was a popular train which originated in Glasgow and ran to Crail; later it was extended to St. Andrews. Originally running on summer Saturdays only, it ran daily during the holiday season. Although suspended during two World Wars, it continued to run until September 1959 when diesel trains took over many of the East Fife operations. The personnel are, left to right: driver David Scott, fireman John Allan, clerk James Lawson, signalman John Clark and guard Robert Harper. The 4-4-0 locomotive number 768 was one of the NBRs crack express locomotives. One of this class was recorded as running the 59.2 miles from Edinburgh Waverley to Dundee in 59 minutes, in the year 1895! Today *express* trains can be allowed up to one hour twenty minutes for the same journey.

High Street Leven in May 1931, with Wemyss & District tramcar number 21 being passed by a small Singer car FG4647 (registered early 1929). The tram actually dated from 1900, and had been built for the Potteries Electric Tramways Company. When that line closed in 1928 it was bought from the scrap dealer E J Walsh (who had been Manager of the small Musselburgh tramway line from 1916 to 1919), who had bought all the tramway stores of the Potteries Company. It was rebuilt to be suitable for the Wemyss line where it gave service until the line closed on 31st January 1932.

The Milton Motor Service was founded by David Eadie from Milton of Balgonie in 1921 operating between Markinch and Leven. His buses were painted in a distinctive canary yellow livery. This is Thornycroft FG2877 of 1927 which in 1932 passed to W Alexander when they acquired the business. Just what the scene in Mitchell Street is supposed to represent is anybody's guess – the rear door was normally for emergency use only – but perhaps it is demonstrating just how the vehicle could be loaded and unloaded simultaneously. Behind to the left is the office of the rival Caley Motor Engineering Company, by that time a subsidiary of the Wemyss tramways undertaking.

…and not a drop was spilled since, fortuitously, the beer bottles demolished by the errant bus were empty! At the corner of Victoria Road and Waggon Road in Leven, the unfortunate incident saw Harris's Thornycroft bus collide with a brewer's dray of empties. The dark green bus was new in June 1931, probably not long before this scene of devastation was recorded. Harris was one of several Leven based bus proprietors and ran to St. Andrews and Anstruther. He was one of the last independent bus operators in the area, holding out against Alexander until eventually absorbed in May 1939, but even after that event he continued to operate tours until the 1950s.

Leven Promenade and the Beach Pavilion in 1964 with an Alexander's bus setting off for Dunfermline. With putting green, amusement park, tennis courts, beach and golf course all at hand, it is no wonder that on this summer day, obviously during the school holidays, the place is buzzing. The unspoiled sweep of six miles of sand round Largo Bay to Earlsferry and Elie is as attractive today as it was then.

Adamson of Leven was a haulage company which entered business in the opposite direction to many of their contemporaries; they converted a charabanc into a lorry, whereas others made a weekday lorry into a weekend charabanc. By 1939 he had three garages servicing a fleet of fifty vehicles. The founder had a major involvement in the road haulage industry and was a founder member of the Fife Hauliers' Association. After the Second World War the company was nationalised, but when denationalisation, then renationalisation followed, the company disappeared for ever.

THE BEACH - ELIE

A governess cart and donkey rides on the sands of Elie beach in the Edwardian era. The sender, May, lets Maggie (the recipient) know that she is "enjoying a very nice holiday at Elie, and we are going a sail on the Steamer today ..", which is a reminder that the Galloway Steam Packet Company ran boats on the Forth until the First World War. Three times a week their excursion steamer, often the *Redgauntlet*, sailed and it was possible to visit the May Island, cruise to Portobello Pier or even steam as far upstream as the Forth Bridge and beyond.

Pittenweem High Street and Market Place in the early 1930s with a distinct lack of road traffic. Other than a single motor car in the distance, the only other vehicle is a horse lorry, standing while a delivery was made. Even then a popular holiday spot, it was also a busy fishing harbour. The wicker basket on the lorry is how families would send luggage in advance, a case or trunk with all the necessities being despatched by rail to the lodgings to await the arrival of the holidaymakers. To this day the harmony of the architecture remains unbroken by any modern intrusion, with the sixteenth century home of the Earls of Kellie on the left, and the street ended by the Tolbooth and Parish Church.

Toll Cross, Pittenweem perhaps sounds grander than the reality, but it is the major crossing of Charles Street over the main A917 road (James Street). On the left the road leads to the railway station, now gone, and commemorated only in the small Station Court housing development. The old (even for then) car heading in that direction is a Wolseley-Siddeley, manufactured for a short period only before the First World War, a collaboration between two men who went separate ways and became better known as individual car manufacturers. Robertson's shop on the left corner no longer exists today.

Auction of the catch at Pittenweem Harbour, before construction of the covered fish market. The auctioneer can be made out at the far side of the crowd, wearing a homburg hat. Observing the scene is a family who appear to be on holiday, the little girl clutching her spade while father carries her bucket; mother seems to be dressed in the latest fashion – at least compared to most of the other on-lookers.

Her Majesty Queen Elizabeth, wife of King George VI visited Pittenweem on 19th September 1950 where she was welcomed by the Provost, James D Lawson who was celebrating having served thirty years on the town council. The royal transport in attendance (a Daimler limousine) has no registration plate, a convention which exists to this day. Shortly after this event the Daimler suffered an unfortunate transmission failure. The Daimler marque was thereafter relegated to the second car, with the premier position taken by a Rolls Royce.

Arrival, courtesy of a team of six horses, of the new lifeboat at Anstruther in July 1904, having been successfully delivered by rail. In September it was named the *James and Mary Walker* and was of the 'Watson' class. This was manned by twelve oarsmen and, remarkably, remained in service until 1933. During this period it was instrumental in the saving of 46 lives.

Pictured at The Shore, Anstruther are three buses belonging to Tom Gardner, whose first garage was in the building at the Harbourhead now occupied by the Scottish Fisheries Museum. Many of Gardner's vehicles were supplied and had bodies built by Peter Crerar of Crieff. He acted as an agent for many 'exotic' makes, and Gardner purchased De Dions, Lancias and at least one Minerva from him, all of which came with Perthshire 'ES' registrations. The nearest vehicle to the photographer is a De Dion with Crerar body. In addition to the Fisheries Museum, Anstruther also has a must-visit award-winning fish and chips shop.